Finding
U
Within You

Rhosheder McHugh

Finding U Within You.
Copyright © 2021. Rhosheder McHugh

Published by:

ISBN: 979-8-7313-4932-1

Dedicated

To you marvelous young man —you were born for a
purpose.
To one lovely young lady— your life was designed
and orchestrated by the Lord.

Acknowledgement

I want to express special thanks to my husband Raye; your prayerful, passionate and purpose-driven attitude has always been a source of inspiration for me and has proven to be a great supply of motivation in accomplishing this task. Your continued encouragement and support has been the engine that propelled me in my quest of writing and releasing this book.

Heartfelt thanks to my son Rai-Judah. You were always there to extend a hug and express your encouragement in simple yet powerful words. You "boosted" me with your enquiring mind and gentle curiosity. All those questions motivated me to extend myself in finding all the possible answers a young mind would need to find the U within them. Son, you were born to Praise the Lord. As I penned this book, I committed you in the Lord's care and it is my heart's desire that your life will manifest these written words.

To my daughter Ra'Myah— my little twin—your continued prayers, as short as they were, touched me indelibly; when you rested your tiny hands on my head and prayed "Jesus, amen", the Lord heard and answered.

Thank you, my baby girl. Continue to pray, little prophetess.

To my parents Clinton & Dianne, I cannot express thanks enough; you are truly my inspiration! Thank you for always asking "when will you finish that book?" Sometimes the human in me got a bit exasperated, but I must admit that your enquiries pushed me to finally accomplish the mission.

Contents

Introduction

Growing up in a Christian home, I learned from a tender age that life can be immensely challenging especially for a young person who is striving to become a better Christian and has the desire to do good. As I grew to learn this, I also realized that as a young person, my youthfulness afforded me the privilege and opportunity to do things other persons could not do. With the guidance of my seniors, I was able to impact and influence the lives of persons in a more efficient and effective way.

I would always disqualify myself from accomplishing more because of my age. From the age of six (6), I began preaching on public transportation— I took pleasure in doing this. To be honest, people were more enthused about listening to a six-year-old exhorter than they were a forty-year-old preacher. I then transitioned from public transportation, to my classrooms and then the pulpit.

People were extremely fascinated and impressed with a girl, who was tremendously passionate and in love with God and His Words. My youthfulness was working for me. What better way to express that God can be a young person's keeper than a young person who gets up and shares it? What I once thought was a "curse" was a blessing!

Being young does not disqualify you; it enhances your chance to be and do great things. While there is a great appreciation for the more mature audience (as they are our best resources of wisdom and experience), youths possess inner and outward strength to do God's work. You are created, designed, and furnished with an inexhaustible volume of vim, vigor and vitality.

God has placed within you the will and zeal to do things that are beyond your mental capacity — He will amaze you! If you put your mind to it, birth the passion and embrace your purpose, you will see the promise come to pass. It is written "...Young man I write unto you because you are strong...!" (St. John 2: 14) You have a task that only you can fulfill. Do not leave this world without emptying your lot. It is time to *Find U within You.*

As a young person, I had to dig deep within to find that part of me that I initially had no interest in. I was, and perhaps still am, a reserved individual. Years ago, when I was in the dawn of my youth, I would compare myself to others; younger, older and my age counterparts and I would disqualify myself from doing whatever task was presented. Without even trying, I just always thought others were better. It was not until one day I was asked to do an impromptu presentation at church. I was almost sure people could hear my heart beating as I walked up to the podium. That is when I began to see my true worth and uniqueness.

My first few sentences flowed better than I thought they would. The more I spoke, the more confident I became. It was at that moment that it dawned on me as I looked at the faces staring at me in amazement that all these people looking at me are just as scared as I was. If they could do what I was doing, they would. I used that as my "aha" moment; "if they could, they would, but I can ... and I am!" As reserved as I was, I spoke from my soul. I gave it my best, and my best proved to be good enough.

When I was through, many people came to me expressing their amazement. Some shared how inspired they were. Some even shared that they could not do what I did. I remember saying from then, at the pivotal age of ten, "...the people looking at you have no reason to judge or criticize you because they are afraid to do it, but you have taken the chance...so just do your best; it is better than doing nothing." This thought has journeyed with me through the years; even to date I still ponder on it and today I am saying it to you, "Unearth the potential that is deep within you, do your best — it is always better than doing nothing. The quest can be daunting, but it is worth it." Let us *find U within You*.

Within every youth there is a unique person to be discovered. There is a U within you. The letter "U" is used informally as an abbreviated version of the word YOU especially among young people when communicating on social media. Interestingly, the letter "U" can easily replace the word 'YOU' because it derives its sound from the letter. The word "YOU" would not be "YOU" without the letter "U". Without the specific letter "U", that word would not have that particular sound. The presence of the letter U is crucial as it is the defining letter in the word.

This mirrors the message of this book, that within you, there is an inner U. Everyone sees you but the world is waiting to be impacted and influenced by U. This inner U gives your life definition and context; it is at your core and is worth exploring so that you can discover and unearth your unique calling and purpose.

The truth is, it did not take me a long time to discover that person within me, however when I did, it was as though I became a brand-new person; my eyes were now open to the understanding that there was more to life than what I knew life to be. This realization impressed upon me in such a powerful way that the inner me was triggered to seek after deeper and more spiritual things.

Being raised in the church, I quickly realized that I was not ordinary— I was a child of the King. Knowing this impacted my outlook in a positive way. I not only accepted this as a thought, but it also became my way of life. I embraced my uniqueness and operated as a child of the King. I knew that in my attempt to make my mark on society, I had to do it from a child of God's perspective. My purpose was not just to touch lives, but to change them. Whether in strides or small steps, I was determined to make my little light shine.

When your passion and youthful exuberance merge, the earth becomes your platform; there is no limit to what God can do through you. God loves young people! He loves you and the youth in you. He does not discriminate; He will use you if you avail yourself to Him.

Being young is a blessing! Being young and fulfilling your purpose in God is an even greater blessing! You have been hand-picked by God for this season to accomplish a task that no one else can. The only door standing between you and attaining that goal is understanding your purpose and unearthing the sparks God has placed within you.

After coming into the knowledge of who I am in God and understanding His appreciation and love for me, I began to work tirelessly for the Kingdom. The drive and push that I had as a youth allowed me, with God's direction, to create ripple effects in my environment. I had a zeal and passion that no one could kill. I was armed with the perspective needed to pull a dying generation to God and an approach that was 'godly-unique'.

I have come to realize that many young people are not aware of how valuable they are not just as a person but even in the Kingdom. Without you, there is no future. Show me youths, and I will show you rare treasures and a future that is bright and flourishing. I want to help you attain self-discovery through my writings.

A popular quote by Kailash Satyarthi, an Indian activist, states "The power of youth is the commonwealth for the entire world. The faces of young people are the faces of our past, our present and our future. No segment in the society can match with the power, idealism, enthusiasm, and courage of the young people." Undoubtedly, youths are the engine of our time. Without youths our future is doomed, there will be little to no progress and growth.

This will be the first of three books in the series *Rip-*

ple Effect, so as we take the journey of discovering self, I implore you to join me as we travel together to *find U within you* so that we can create positive and lasting effects and impact on those who will cross our paths.

At the end of each chapter is a special scripture passage carefully selected as a supporting resource to help you gain more biblical insight so that you can apply the Word of God in your pursuit to *find the U within you*.

Young man, young lady, the world is awaiting your impact. Find that critical U within you and watch the Lord do wonders with and through you.

Chapter 1
He Made the Earth & You

One of my most frequently used statements is, "the Lord makes no mistake." He never says "oops," "sorry" or "oh my I made a mistake." Everything the Lord does is well done. He saw the need to make an investment in time. He saw the need to fashion man, and not just any man; He saw the need to make you and me.

As a child, I always heard that the hand of the Lord was upon my life. Even though I heard it so often, I really did not grasp the depth of that statement until I became more mature. After careful reflection and examination, I realized that the Lord was assembling all the puzzle pieces of my life together. I was gainfully employed in His service— called and chosen for a special purpose. The Almighty God created and fashioned you, yes you, for a marvelous purpose.

You are special, you are important, you are relevant, and you are designed and fashioned by the Almighty God. When the Lord created this earth, He had you in mind. He knew what your personality would be. He knew what your complexion would be. He knows what you enjoy and what you despise.

Nothing about you takes the Lord by surprise. Even when you are at your weakest, He knows. Yes! He is very much aware of your faults— the darkest most alarming secret He knows and even then, He still loves you and still has His hands upon you.

As a child there was a song that I always sang, *"I am so glad that Jesus loves me...Jesus loves even me."* Tears would fill my eyes when I thought about the fact that of all the people in the world (7.8 billion), Jesus still saw me worthy enough to be loved and sees me as a precious jewel in his sight.

Even you, He took the time to carve, mold and make you. As a young female, I thought I was never good enough. I despised my image, my shape, as I always thought being "slim" was the defining look of a beautiful young lady. I was quite curvaceous. I thought God did not love me to make me this way, so I tried to shy away from being seen— always thinking I was never good enough. As time progressed, I realized that I was more than just what could be seen; deep within that shapely form was a heart of gold that God had taken quality time to design. There was more to me than just my external features. Before I emerged from my mother's womb, God had it all figured out; how I would look, my features, my organs and cells, down to the minutest detail of my DNA. He did not confuse me with my cousins, friends, and neighbors. He made me intentionally.

With all the complexities of the earth, and all the concerns of the world, the Lord has found time to concern Himself about your wellbeing. You are not just an irrelevant piece placed in the game of life, but you are a masterpiece in God's hands. He created the earth and He created you.

The truth is, once you can understand that you are not just a part of the whole but rather an essential part of the puzzle, designed and hand-picked by God, the way you think, act, and believe will be impacted. You were not just a random pick, the Lord spent quality time on you. The fact that you crossed His mind implies how valuable you are.

Have you fully grasped the enormity of God's love and value of you? Inhale...exhale.

The fact that you are alive, breathing the breath God has created is an indication that He cares for you. While navigating the big things, He thought it essential to allow you to wake up, to open your eyes and experience a new day— to function and carry out your purpose simply because YOU are necessary.

While the universe at large is relevant, without you— God's prized possession— it would not be the same. The Lord created not just the earth, but He took quality time to create you. He had you in mind before you were even conceived. Strategically placed in a specific location and situation, is a treasure created in God's image and likeness; an investment made by God. The earth awaits the U that the Lord has spent time to invest in.

According to the National Association for Gifted Children, "No gifted individual is exactly the same, each with his own unique patterns and traits," and as such we patiently await the blooming of the unique abilities and talents that are embedded in U.

Let us dig into the Word

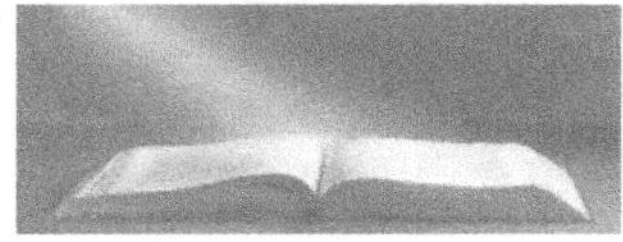

1. How do these scriptures apply to you?

2. How do they make you feel about yourself?

3. What do they say to you about the value God places on you?

Take some time to personalize them based on the readings from chapter 1.

Genesis 1:26 ESV

Then God said, "Let Us make man in Our image, according to Our likeness; and let them rule over the fish of the sea and over the birds of the sky and over the cattle and over all the earth, and over every creeping thing that creeps on the earth."

Genesis 2:7
And the Lord God formed man of the dust of the ground and breathed into his nostrils the breath of life; and man became a living soul.

Job 33:4 NKJV
The Spirit of God has made me, and the breath of the
Almighty gives me life.

Psalm 139:13 ESV
For you formed my inward parts; you knitted me together in my mother's womb.

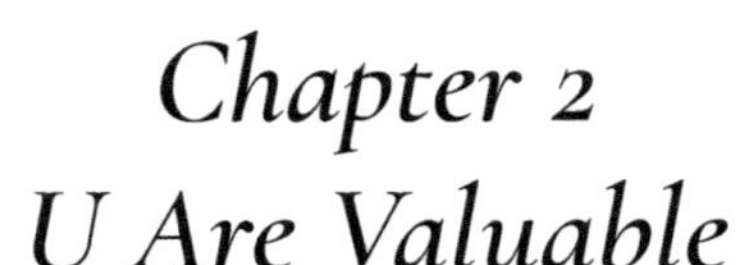

Chapter 2
U Are Valuable

As a child, I always knew my worth. However, in understanding my worth, I first had to understand that my worth and quality could only be found in the One who created me. If I received a gift from someone and had difficulty figuring out how it functioned, chances are I would reach out to the person after checking the instructions and if all fails, ultimately, I would have to connect with the manufacturer.

The creator always has the answers. Now, if you are having struggles trying to understand your worth, your value, what exactly your life entails there is no better person to turn to than our Creator. Let me insert this necessary point right here; YOU ARE GOD'S HIGHEST ELEMENT OF CREATION. This is evident because you were carved in His image and likeness. God did not create you based on an idea He had, or a drawing He made. He took time to shape you in His image and likeness. He values you so much that He has crowned you with glory and honor! You are not just an "it," you are God's masterpiece! Youths, please walk with your head held high, you are not just an ordinary person; your name is known by the Most High God!

While earthly beings might not recognize you, the Creator of heaven and earth, the One who sculpted this earth, took some time out of his routine to etch and make an indelible impression on earth by bringing you into you.

You are not cheap, you are priceless! Perhaps you have been overlooked by men, perhaps no one knows your name or even remembers you, but God knows every detail about you. He never confuses you with anyone— He knows the number of strands of hair on your head! I dare say if the Sovereign God knows about you, then you are of great worth!

You are not an accident my friend. You and your affairs matter to God!

Let me share with you an article that I wrote to the Editor of a local newspaper relating an experience I had some years ago in Jamaica.

Although it is directed to young ladies, young men, please note that you are just as valuable and relevant. Never let anyone underestimate you and take you for granted. You are valuable.

LETTER OF THE DAY –
'I'm not cheap; I'm a lady!'
Published: Sunday | June 22, 2008
The Editor, Sir:
WHILE WALKING on the road one day, I overheard a conversation among youths my age, or probably older, two guys and a girl.

These were the lines I caught: (apparently the question was directed to Guy 2)
Girl " ... so she's not your bonifide?" translated:
"...so she's not your girlfriend?"

Guy 1 " ... watch ya, not at all" translated:
"oh no, not at all"

Guy 2 " ... no sah, she ... (hiss teeth)" translated:
"she? oh no!"

Girl "I coulda swear she a yuh wife, so she a wah" translated:
"I was almost sure she was the special lady in your life, what then is her status?"

Guy 2 "she ah borrowed goods" translated:
"She is just borrowed goods."
Girl " ... oh cool ... "

Borrowed goods.

Ladies, women, girls, gals - females - whichever category you place yourself, no guy has the right to 'style' or refer to you as borrowed goods, well that's if you don't give him reasons to. The above lines in the conversation disturbed me, I'm by no means feminist, but I mean, what exactly is it that men see females as?

The word 'borrowed' refers to being on loan or for rent; goods can be seen as possessions. Putting them together, the guy was actually stating that the girl he apparently was or is involved with is not his possession, he is just renting her; she's simply a loan.

I really don't know if I should blame the girl or the guy but let me say this much.

I don't know about most of you, but I can speak for myself and some of the women I know. I consider myself very expensive. There is a high cost for me, I am not cheap. Guys can't buy me with words or regular lyrics or even their looks.

Supreme Being

I am not like novels, clothes or even food that you can pick up off the shelf - I am rare. There's only one me. I cannot be shared, and I will not be distributed. I consider myself a jewel; I don't care if you don't see me that way. What matters most to me are my name and my attribute. What people think about me based on facts and not what is heard.

If I don't put myself on a pinnacle, no one else will.

Woman was extracted from man. Everything else was made

by words but the Supreme Being did a special work on the female species, carved by His Hands - which is a clear indication that we are not normal, we nuh cheap! It's rude for someone to refer to us - as borrowed goods!

Live as ladies. Let men search and work hard to win you, Christian ladies. As the saying goes, "we must be so well hidden in Christ that a man has to go real deep in God to find us"!

Ladies put a price on yourself. You are expensive! Well, if you all don't want to accept that fact then I will - I am expensive, and I am not for sale, neither am I on a loan or for rent!

Any guy who gets me, gets a treasure. Tell yourself that ladies and act it.

Much love to you all. Be what God created you to be ... a lady!

In as much as the young lady is precious, young men, you too are prized and treasured. You are more than your external features; you are more than possessions and what you must give a girl, the U within you is valuable and is waiting to be discovered.

Let us dig into the Word:

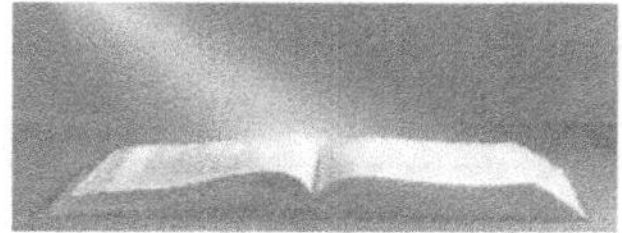

1. How Do These Scriptures Apply to You?

2. How do they make you feel about yourself?

3. What do they say to you about the value God places on you?

Take some time to personalize them; based on the readings from the chapter2.

Ephesians 2: 4-7 NKJV
But God, who is rich in mercy, because of His great love with which He loved us, even when we were dead in trespasses, made us alive together with Christ ... that in the ages to come He might show the exceeding riches of His grace in His kindness toward us in Christ Jesus

1 Peter 1:18-19

Forasmuch as ye know that ye were not redeemed with corruptible things, as silver and gold ...But with the precious blood of Christ, as of a lamb without blemish and without spot:

____

____

____

____

____

____

____

____

____

____

____

____

Luke 12:24 NKJV
Consider the ravens: They do not sow or reap, they have no storeroom or barn; yet God feeds them. And how much more valuable you are than birds!

1 Peter 2:9
But ye are a chosen generation, a royal priesthood, an holy nation, a peculiar people; that ye should shew forth the praises of him who hath called you...

____

____

____

____

____

____

____

____

____

____

____

____

____

Exodus 19:5
Now therefore, if ye will obey my voice indeed, and keep my covenant, then ye shall be a peculiar treasure unto me above all people: for all the earth is mine:

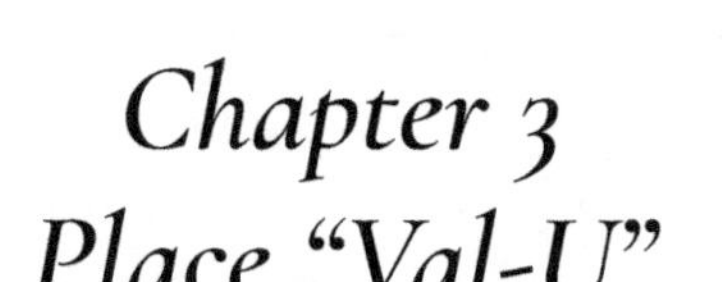

Chapter 3
Place "Val-U"

There was a little Israelite girl who was taken into captivity by a powerful man called Naaman and his Syrian Army. Naaman was the captain of the army; however, though powerful, he had a malady— he was a leper. Now let us take some time to process this. This little girl was a slave. She was in a strange country, around strangers yet she was not daunted by the events and the people around her. She knew of Naaman's predicament, she knew he was her enemy. She also knew of the power of God, and even in her unfortunate situation, she did not keep this information to herself. Her position and place at that moment was for a purpose. This little girl despite her pain capitalized on her position and used the information she had and made a valuable contribution to the life of her master.

Her divine positioning took precedence over her pain. She dug deep within herself, found her inner person and allowed her heart to extend love even though she was a slave, and no doubt resented her status. Evidently, her place "val-U" meant more to her. Though I may not appreciate how I got here and why I am here, the fact is I am already here so might as well be a blessing.

The prickly truth is, God really does not need you. He does not need your assistance or aid. God can do it all by Himself. However, he loves you and has placed you here for a purpose. Has the thought ever dawned on you that you are where you are because God wants you there?

That family that you were born in, the community that you reside in, that school that you are attending or attended, that college class that you may have, that course you are dreading, being placed next to that co-worker who is driving you nuts, it was all in the scope of God's mind.

You were placed there because there is a task for you to do. God does not place his prized possession—you — at a random location without having any purpose or aim in mind. As God's possession, as His masterpiece, you are where you are for His glory and His divine will. Go ahead and take authority over the space; get comfortable knowing that God has placed you there and you have a job to do.

What is the point of having authority and dominion and not applying it to better the space that God has placed you in? You are where you are because God sees within you the ability to transform, alter, correct and fix your arena. Do not be daunted by your surroundings, shake yourself, understand your purpose, understand the right God has given to you then activate and perform the tasks you have been entrusted with!

You can do it my purpose-driven friend!

Come on young lady, young man; remember, you were bought with a price!

You are not where you are as a placeholder; you are divinely positioned by God to do a work. Yes, right there in your family, right there in your church, your community, your workplace and even your school. Anywhere you find yourself my friend, if you are walking in the will of the Lord, God has set you up to do a work.

You are divinely positioned by God, invade your place and space with the strength of your inner you.

Let us dig into the Word:

1. How do these scriptures apply to you?

2. How do they make you feel about yourself?

3. What do they say to you about the value God places on you?

Take some time to personalize them based on the readings from chapter 3.

Romans 8:28
And we know that all things work together for good to them that love God, to them who are the called according to his purpose.

Psalm 37:23
The steps of a good man are ordered by the Lord: and he delighteth in his way.

Philippians 1:6
Being confident of this very thing, that he which hath begun a good work in you will perform it until the day of Jesus Christ:

____

____

____

____

____

____

____

____

____

____

____

____

____

Chapter 4
Won...Two...Three...Passion!

Understanding who you are to God, who you are in God and where He has placed you, can be likened to starting the ignition of a car. You are now ready and raring to go!

God has a vessel who understands its position, worth and value and sees everyone else as a potential and suitable candidate to be a vessel of honor ready for God's use. Young man! Young lady! Knowing your value is imperative; but it is not sufficient to just know and not operate accordingly. Such a position can be qualified as one who is a part of a soccer team but is always benched or always reserved and never gets involved in the action. Simply making the team but always sitting on the sidelines is not enough. A valuable team player is considered as playing a part on the field, actively participating, scoring goals, falling sometimes but getting up— running with the ball and getting your hands "dirty."

There is a difference when you are an active participant, when you get in the game and you win, not just once or twice, but consistently. It becomes a lifestyle, and you are zealous about winning until it becomes second nature to win.

Win? Win what? To find your fulfillment in Christ, to understand He positioned you for greatness will stir within you a passion to win souls for the Kingdom. As a young person, the best thing you could possibly do in your lifetime is to live for God and work for Him. As a worker, your goal is to enjoy winning souls for God. You should be a magnet, like Esther. She was positioned in the office of a Queen to carry out a distinct and critical purpose. There was a specific assignment for her to do. Like her, the Lord has deposited within you the tools, the will, and the power to minister to souls. God has placed you at that spot, yes, on that bus, at that supermarket, at that very moment to accomplish one thing— to win souls.

When you have come into a clear understanding of who you are and whose you are, you will then testify "I have won ... two, three souls for the Lord - and I am not through yet; my passion has been stirred." A car with the engine running but remaining in a parked position serves little to no purpose, but when you get the vehicle moving, accelerate, drive along the path, keep pressing and testifying to the passengers you have gathered along the way, it becomes a most valuable asset. That is you, a useful vehicle winning souls for the Lord.

Unearth that gift and passion to serve the One who created the world. Avail yourself and allow Him to steer you on the path to won...two...three souls for His Kingdom.

Let us dig into the Word:

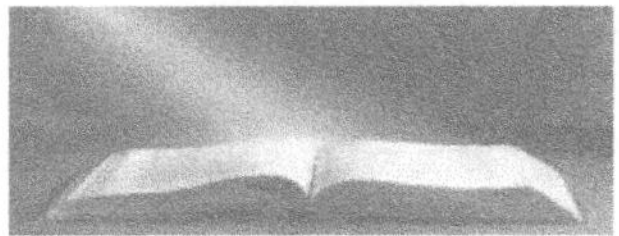

1. How do these scriptures apply to you?
2. How do they make you feel about yourself?
3. What do they say to you about the value God places on you?

Take some time to personalize them based on the readings from chapter 4.

Proverbs 10:5
He that gathereth in summer is a wise son: but he that sleep-
eth in harvest is a son that causeth shame.

Acts 1:8

But ye shall receive power, after that the Holy Ghost is come upon you: and ye shall be witnesses unto me both in Jerusalem, and in all Judaea, and in Samaria, and unto the uttermost part of the earth.

Proverbs 11:30
The fruit of the righteous is a tree of life; and he that win-
neth souls is wise.

II Corinthians 5:11
Knowing, therefore, the terror of the Lord, we persuade men....

Chapter 5
Without "YOU" We Just Have "Th"

You have an inexhaustible supply of potential! You have what it takes to achieve the greatest. You may not have the finances or all the resources you believe you need, but you have the strength, the vigor, the vim, and the vitality! Can I state the obvious? Without 'you', there is no <u>you</u>th! Without youths there will be no future.

The Lord absolutely loves young people! YOU are crucial to the growth of the body of Christ. You represent not just a power force in culture and commerce, but you are also the most essential resource to advancing the Kingdom of God. The Bible is filled with myriads of youthful examples that the Lord used in a potent manner to express this fact. He does not discriminate against age, but has a treasured spot for young people...If you are available, God has an opening!

Being young makes you a suitable candidate for more reasons than one:

- You can relate to your own generation more than individuals of previous generations.
- You can connect with your peers.
- **You can bring "life" to the Ministry.**
- You see what others overlook.
- You have energy and strength to your advantage.
- You consider others' perspectives.
- You put the U in youth.

According to a 2019 survey conducted by the RE:NEW Youth Ministry, youths were asked the reasons that allowed them to willingly open up to youth workers.

The following is their response:

- approachable
- helping
- understanding
- able to build a deep connection
- trustworthy
- capable

There is a magnetic compelling force that pulls youngsters to each other. You can connect and relate on a level that others cannot.

I understand youths are bombarded and inundated

with many challenges that sometimes can make them indecisive. But youths are also filled with an undeniable and impressive measure of excitement and zeal that can create a ripple effect in the world. If this passion and enthusiasm is fostered and nurtured in a godly manner, there is nothing that can withstand a youth armed and ready to serve the Lord!

You have what it takes; you are a crucial member of the team. Every Paul needs a Timothy.

You are the Timothy that your church has been waiting on!

Let us dig into the Word:

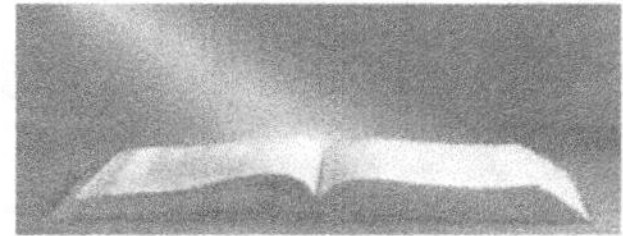

1. How do these scriptures apply to you?
2. How do they make you feel about yourself?
3. What do they say to you about the value God places on you?

Take some time to personalize them based on the readings from chapter 5.

1 Timothy 4:12
Let no man despise thy youth; but be thou an example of the believers, in word, in conversation, in charity, in spirit, in faith, in purity.

Psalm 127:3-5
Lo, children are an heritage of the Lord: and the fruit of the womb is his reward. As arrows are in the hand of a mighty man; so are children of the youth. Happy is the man that hath his quiver full of them: they shall not be ashamed, but they shall speak with the enemies in the gate.

1 Samuel 17: 33 -36
And Saul said to David, Thou art not able to go against this Philistine to fight with him: for thou art but a youth, and he a man of war from his youth. And David said unto Saul, Thy servant kept his father's sheep, and there came a lion, and a bear, and took a lamb out of the flock: And I went out after him, and smote him, and delivered it out of his mouth: and when he arose against me, I caught him by his beard, and smote him, and slew him. Thy servant slew both the lion and the bear: and this uncircumcised Philistine shall be as one of them, seeing he hath defied the armies of the living God.

1 John 2: 14

I have written unto you, fathers, because ye have known him that is from the beginning. I have written unto you, young men, because ye are strong, and the word of God abideth in you, and ye have overcome the wicked one.

Chapter 6
U Can do All Things!

As time progresses and you experience growth, you will realize that things and life will become more challenging. There is no smooth sailing road in life. The reality is, there are some potholes and sometimes you will have to detour, other times you will have to pause, retry and go again. Whatever condition may present itself —never give up! You have what it takes to win!

There will be many distractors and detractors and you may sometimes lose your footing, but never lose sight of the goal that is ahead. While the enemy sets his plans, plots and ploys, you must remember your purpose, passion and power. Though you may appear to be alone, God has invested much within you; hence, you are well able to withstand the darts thrown at you. It would be unrealistic to say you will not receive blows, it would also be absurd to say no challenges will come, but never take your foot off the pedal. Blaze the course and go and fulfill that which you have been called and equipped and dispatched to do.

You have one purpose, one task, and that is to do the will of the Lord. The race must go on. There will always be persons standing by the sidelines— do not allow them to distract you but keep your eyes fastened on the prize.

Ready...

Set....

Blaze...!

As you blaze for the Lord, sparks will be left behind you. The intent is that someone will see the spark and rightfully, it takes just a spark to get the fire flaring! You will leave trails of seeds behind and someone will come along and allow it to germinate within their soul.

Young man, young lady, asa you are now aware of how essential you are to God, to yourself and to ministry, it is time. The time is now to get ready, set and blaze! U can do it! U can do all things; your greatest challenge is yourself. Let go and allow the inner U to bloom. Shed the facade and allow God's light to feed your inner self, so that U can emanate and spread ripples to those in your sphere of influence.

Kofi Annan, Ghanian diplomat, pens it best writing "Young people should be at the forefront of global change and innovation. Empowered, they can be key agents for development and peace. If, however, they are left on society's margins, all of us will be impoverished..." The world awaits the influence of its most treasured resources - the youths.

Let us dig into the Word:

1. How do these scriptures apply to you?

2. How do they make you feel about yourself?

3. What do they say to you about the value God places on you?

Take some time to personalize them based on the readings from chapter 6.

Psalm 37:4
Delight yourself also in the LORD, And He shall give you the desires of your heart.

Psalm 16:11
Thou wilt shew me the path of life: in thy presence is fulness of joy; at thy right hand there are pleasures for evermore.

____

____

____

____

____

____

____

____

____

____

____

____

____

Colossians 3:23
And whatsoever ye do, do it heartily, as to the Lord, and not unto men

John 9:4
We must work the works of Him who sent me as long as it is day; night is coming when no one can work.

———

Chapter 7
Time to Unearth U

Have you ever taken a trip, or returned from a long expedition and instead of unpacking your luggage you "live" out of your suitcase? For some people, the task of unpacking can be overwhelming. Many resign to what seems to be the most convenient course of action, which is unpacking as the need arises for each item. Since these items are not in their usual place, over time people become flustered with the difficulty of locating items because they have become so accustomed to living out of a box.

Similarly, when you restrict yourself and do not live up to your full potential, you stifle your spiritual growth and progress and hinder your ability to unearth and find the *U within you.* Choosing the path that is easiest may seem like a good idea at the time but will ultimately lead to frustration as you find you have stifled your ability to grow. Rather than looking at the scope of possibilities, you end up confined in your narrow perception of yourself and your capabilities.

You deserve to be the best version of you and the

world is waiting to be impacted by that which has been deposited in you. I propose a challenge — do not leave this world without making a lasting and impactful mark.

Now that you have been alerted, informed, and educated about the 'U' within you, there is work for you to do! Yes youths, there is great vocation awaiting your expertise. The world is waiting on you to catch up to the reality that there is a position with your name assigned to it, a task unique and designed specifically for you.

To say everything will be smooth sailing is a fib, but to say you have what it takes to overcome is a fact. With God by your side, you are well able to withstand all the storms that come your way. Let nothing and no one derail you from your purpose.

Keep your eyes, mind and heart fixated on Jesus. The Lord kept David who was only a shepherd boy, Joseph who was hated by his brothers, the Girl who was only Naaman's servant, Esther who was only a Hebrew maiden amongst other youths of the Bible, and I can assure you that He will keep you. You are special enough! You are His prized possession! You are the apple of His eyes! Unearth your potential in God and He will release His power in you!

No good master would entrust all and sundry with his treasured gift; he will only trust you if he believes that you have what it takes to build on what is precious to him, and what he deems to be valuable. If the Lord saw the need to invest in you— His most precious gift— then it means that He trusts and believes in you to respond and react when He speaks and instructs. He believes in you to be His servant. When you discover that He is your master, your will becomes embodied in His will and ultimately your resolve will not matter but only His will for your life.

Let us dig into the Word:

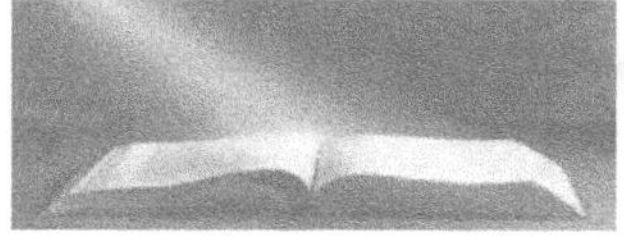

1. How do these Scriptures apply to you?

2. How do they make you feel about yourself?

3. What do they say to you about the value God places on you?

Take some time to personalize them based on the readings from chapter 7.

1 Timothy 4:15 TLB
Put these abilities to work; throw yourself into your tasks so that everyone may notice your improvement and progress.

Colossians 3:23
And whatsoever ye do, do it heartily, as to the Lord, and not unto men

Proverbs 19:21
There are many devices in a man's heart; nevertheless the counsel of the Lord, that shall stand.

Romans 8:28
And we know that all things work together for good to them that love God, to them who are the called according to his purpose.

73

____

____

____

____

____

____

____

____

____

____

____

____

____

Chapter 8
David the Beloved

Now that we have gotten to this point of unearthing who we are, it would help if we could mirror our lives to someone with whom we may be quite familiar with from the Bible— David the beloved. David was the youngest of eight sons of Jesse. He was overlooked by his father and underestimated by his brothers. Born in an average household, he had no kingly connections. He could always be found in the fields, tending to his father's flock. He was seen by all (including himself) as a regular child; one who had little idea of how drastically his life would change because of understanding the weight that was placed on his life by God.

His primary job description was to tend the sheep. His life was exceedingly basic and average. His associates and family did not think much of him. His marvelous character was yet to be witnessed by the world. However, heaven and the beasts he tended were privy to his inner 'U'. They were aware of the hours he spent in prayer and praise as he played his harp and sang praises to God in the wilderness.

The beauty of God is that He can take even someone from a place of lowliness and implant a gift within them. Only you, coupled with your trust and confidence in Him, can extract and demonstrate that gift that is in you. Your beginning does not define your ending; your condition is not your conclusion. Your life has been orchestrated by God and His plans for you are so much greater than what your eyes or anyone around you can see NOW.

On a regular day, David was out in the field, conducting his affairs as was expected. It is interesting to note that David enjoyed his responsibilities; while doing his chores, he would steal away time to bask in the presence of God. David, the beloved, was not so completely consumed by his work that he could not find time to meditate on God. Even whilst doing his chores, he saw the need to tap into his source of survival.

Interestingly, one day while he was doing his work, he was summoned from the field by the Prophet Samuel. Perhaps David thought, "they just need some water from the well or maybe some questions about the sheep." However, what he perceived as an ordinary day, unfolded into a day that would change the trajectory of his life and impact the lives of all of us today. The ruddy shepherd boy was sent for and it was in this moment he transitioned from just a shepherd boy to being anointed King of Israel.

Wait...

Let us take a step back!

That was a remarkably immense transition in just a few moments. So, let us recap: David, a shepherd boy, rejected by his dad, underrated by his siblings, unqualified for any other job but a sheep tender was in a snap... Anointed to become KING!!

While it may have been a surprise to everyone in David's family circle, I can only imagine how he was as he mentally recounted the moments he spent with God and how those moments strengthened him. Certainly, God had deposited within him an incomprehensible astronomical quantity of favor while he stole away in His presence. You see, it really does not matter how others see you; you must understand that others cannot define you. Your life is shaped and molded by how you see yourself and your acceptance of how God sees you.

When you understand how God sees you -

A Bear is no match for you.

A Lion is like a harmless cat.

Goliath is like a dwarf.

A slingshot is like a high-powered weapon.

The Philistines army is like a colony of ants running around.

When you understand what He has invested in you -

A Bear is no match for you.

A Lion is a walk in the park.

Goliath is not a giant in your eyes.

A slingshot is a powerful tool.

The Philistines army is like a colony of

ants just running around without their

heads.

Oh yes, sounds repetitive? That is because understanding how God sees us, is accepting and embracing what He has invested in us. It is seeing the impossible as possible. It is seeing things through the lens of the divine. It is seeing the magnanimity of your potential and the mammoth capacity He has created you with. In simple terms: it is *Finding U within you,* and this is worth reiterating.

There is much more within you.

You are not an 'oops'! You are not a mistake!

You were created with God's plans for you in mind. You were not created by chance— You are formed by God's design. David, the beloved, was able to unmask who He was and find himself within himself because He understood God's position in his life.

Youths, understanding God's position and **finding u within you** is a hurdle that David crossed over and the intent of this book is to get you to cross that obstacle too.

As you get over that hurdle, there will be many other hurdles ahead, one such is **finding and functioning** *in your rightful place* - this will be discussed in the second book in this series, where Queen Esther helps us to understand more about purpose in our positions, but to get there, we first must discover who we are.

As you begin your journey, here are a handful of my thoughts that you might find helpful:

<u>Take some time to personalize them; make them applicable on your journey to finding U within you.</u>

"I don't fear tomorrow because my God already worked out my tomorrow yesterday."

____

____

____

____

____

____

"God thought about me today; I'm still alive."

____

____

____

____

____

______

"To please everyone is to fail yourself."

____

____

____

____

____

____

"To make an excuse is to be lazy."

____

____

____

____

____

____

"Even dirt is significant, man was made from it."

____

____

———

"The stones and rocks in our way are not intended to be obstacles but should be used as foundations to boost us."

———

"The seed(s) you plant today will grow to become the tree your children will eat from."

———

"Your condition does not determine your conclusion. God IS bringing you out! "

____

____

____

____

———

"As bad as it may seem; God is still present."

____

____

____

____

____

———

About the Author

Rhosheder McHugh is a trained Educator and Literacy Specialist. She is a graduate of Shortwood Teachers' College in Jamaica, Monroe Community College & Roberts Wesleyan College in the United States.

Rhosheder resides in Rochester NY. She serves as a minister at Praise Sanctuary Ministries International Apostolic, under the leadership of Bishop and Lady Raye McHugh, Sr.

She takes pleasure in ministering to young people. Her passion is to influence and impact the lives of youths in a positive way.

As she strives to create positive ripples in the lives of young people, she hopes to take them on a journey through her writings and life experiences, expressing and demonstrating that being young is a blessing and advocating that all youths have a gift within them that the world is waiting on; but this can be attained only if they first appreciate their 'YOU-niqueness' and who they are in God.

Rhosheder met and fell in love with Raye McHugh Jr., her husband of 8 years. Their union has produced two beautiful children: Rai-Judah and Ra'Myah.

Rhosheder McHugh is the Author of the series *The*

Ripple Effect.